# ARTIFICIAL INTELLIGENCE IN MUSIC

*Blending Creativity and Technology*

## Sarnia de la Mare

**Tale Teller Club**

# CONTENTS

Standard Dreams


In my gothic dreams I am a dark princess
with a pet bat and obviously a
a black cat

I can cast hideous spells
on men (and women) who wrong me
because it isn't fine
when they are mean to me online

Trolls die as soon as they leave the building
straight under a bus
no fuss
for I have the power
just one look
can make them cower

In my pink dreams I am an angel
who forgives, feeds the poor
always gives with wings
of love
plus, I sing
mostly on a cloud
floating
randomly
from above


©2024 Sarnia de la Maré FRSA

# Artificial Intelligence in Music: Blending Creativity and Technology by Sarnia de la Maré FRSA

# CHAPTER 1: INTRODUCTION TO ARTIFICIAL INTELLIGENCE IN MUSIC

## The Evolution of Artificial Intelligence in the Music Industry

Artificial intelligence (AI) has become an integral part of our daily lives, transforming various industries and sectors. The music industry, too, has witnessed the rapid evolution of AI, revolutionizing the way music is created, produced, and consumed. In this subchapter, we will delve into the fascinating journey of AI in the music industry, exploring its impact on creative arts practitioners.

AI-generated art in the music industry has emerged as a game-changer, enabling artists to explore new dimensions of creativity. Using machine learning algorithms, AI can analyze vast amounts of musical data, identifying patterns and generating compositions that captivate and inspire. This technology empowers musicians to experiment with novel sounds, harmonies, and structures, pushing the boundaries of traditional music genres. Creative arts practitioners can now harness AI tools to compose unique pieces, blending their artistic vision with the computational capabilities of AI.

Moreover, AI has facilitated the democratization of music production. Previously, access to professional recording studios and expensive equipment limited many aspiring artists. However, AI-powered software and applications now allow anyone to create and produce high-quality music from the comfort of their own homes. This democratization has opened doors for emerging talents, fostering a more diverse and inclusive music industry.

Beyond composition and production, AI has also transformed the way music is consumed and enjoyed. Recommendation systems powered by AI algorithms analyze individual preferences and behaviours, curating personalized playlists for listeners. This enhances the discovery of new artists and genres, expanding the exposure of creative arts practitioners to wider audiences. Additionally, AI-driven platforms enable music streaming services to predict and adapt to individual tastes, creating a more immersive and engaging experience for listeners.

While AI has made significant strides in the music industry, its impact extends beyond sound. AI in photography and visual arts has revolutionized the creation and manipulation of visual content. With AI-powered image recognition and analysis, artists can now generate stunning visuals, automate image editing, and create immersive experiences. This fusion of AI and visual arts provides creative arts practitioners with powerful tools to express their artistic visions in unprecedented ways.

In conclusion, the evolution of artificial intelligence in the music industry has revolutionized the creative landscape for arts practitioners. From AI-generated compositions to democratized music production and personalized listening experiences, AI has opened new avenues for creativity and innovation. Furthermore, the integration of AI in photography and visual arts has expanded the possibilities of visual expression. As AI continues to evolve, creative arts practitioners can embrace this technology as a powerful ally in their artistic journeys, blending creativity and technology to create awe-inspiring works of art.

# DEFINING AI-GENERATED ART IN MUSIC

In recent years, the advancement of artificial intelligence (AI) has permeated various industries, transforming the way we live, work, and create. The creative arts industry has also witnessed the impact of AI, particularly in the realm of music. This subchapter aims to provide a comprehensive understanding of AI-generated art in music, exploring its implications, possibilities, and challenges.

AI-generated art in the music industry has emerged as a thrilling frontier, blending the realms of technology and creativity. Essentially, it involves the use of AI algorithms to compose, produce, and even perform music. These algorithms are designed to analyze vast amounts of musical data, including genre-specific patterns, harmonic progressions, and melodic structures. By employing machine learning techniques, AI systems can then generate original compositions or offer suggestions to human artists, enhancing their creative process. Artificial Intelligence in Artificial Intelligence in Music: Blending Creativity and Technology One of the key advantages of AI-generated art in music is its ability to explore uncharted territories. AI algorithms can break free from conventional compositional techniques, pushing boundaries and offering novel musical experiences. This opens up a world of possibilities for both artists and listeners, fostering innovation and experimentation in the music industry.

However, the integration of AI in music creation also poses several challenges. Critics argue that AI-generated music lacks the emotional depth and authenticity that human artists bring to their work. While AI algorithms can learn from existing musical patterns, they struggle to capture the intangible aspects of human expression, such as personal experiences and emotions. As a result, there is an ongoing debate about the role of AI in creative arts and whether it can truly replace human artistry.

Beyond the realm of music, AI has also made significant strides in photography and visual arts. AI-powered image recognition and editing tools have revolutionized the way photographers and visual artists work. From automated image tagging to intelligent retouching, AI algorithms can streamline and enhance the creative process, saving time and expanding artistic possibilities. Artificial Intelligence in Music: Blending Creativity and Technology

However, concerns about AI-generated art in photography and visual arts also arise. Some argue that relying too heavily on AI tools can lead to a homogenization of artistic styles, as algorithms tend to favor popular trends. Additionally, questions about copyright and ownership arise when AI is involved in the creation process. Who owns the rights to an AI-generated artwork: the artist, the AI developer, or the AI system itself?

As AI continues to evolve, it is crucial for creative arts practitioners to embrace and understand its potential impact on their respective fields. By exploring the nuances of AI-generated art in music, photography, and visual arts, artists can navigate the intersection of creativity and technology, harnessing AI as a powerful tool to augment their artistic vision. The future of AI-generated art is still unfolding, and it is up to artists to shape its trajectory, ensuring that it serves as a catalyst for innovation rather than a replacement for human creativity.

# THE IMPACT OF AI ON THE CREATIVE ARTS PRACTITIONERS

In recent years, Artificial Intelligence (AI) has revolutionized various industries, and the creative arts field is no exception. This subchapter explores the profound impact of AI on creative arts practitioners, specifically focusing on AI-generated art in the music industry and the use of AI in photography and visual arts.

AI-generated art in the music industry has opened up a world of possibilities for musicians, composers, and producers. With AI algorithms capable of analyzing vast amounts of data and learning patterns, they can now create unique compositions and melodies that push the boundaries of creativity. AI can also assist in the composition process by generating harmonies, chord progressions, and even complete songs, providing artists with a wealth of inspiration and new ideas to explore.

Moreover, AI technology has also proven to be a valuable tool for musicians in enhancing their performances. AI-powered virtual assistants can provide real-time feedback and suggestions, helping performers refine their technique and interpretation. This collaboration between human musicians and AI algorithms has the potential to elevate live performances to new heights, blurring the lines between human creativity and machine intelligence.

In the realm of photography and visual arts, AI has introduced new avenues for creativity and expression. AI algorithms can now analyze and understand visual content, enabling automated editing, image enhancement, and even the creation of entirely new artworks. Artists can leverage AI to experiment with different styles, seamlessly blend elements from various photographs, or generate entirely new visual concepts that push the boundaries of traditional artistic techniques.

Furthermore, AI can also assist artists in the curation and organization of their art collections. By using machine learning algorithms, artists can efficiently manage and categorize their vast libraries of images, making it easier to discover and utilize their work in various creative projects.

While AI offers numerous advantages to creative arts practitioners, it also raises important questions about the role of human creativity in an increasingly automated world. As AI becomes more integrated into the creative process, artists must navigate a delicate balance between utilizing AI as a tool to enhance their creativity and maintaining their unique artistic vision.

In conclusion, the impact of AI on creative arts practitioners cannot be overstated. The emergence of AI-generated art in the music industry and the integration of AI in photography and visual arts have ushered in a new era of creativity and innovation. By embracing AI as a collaborator and tool, creative arts practitioners can unlock new realms of artistic expression and push the boundaries of their craft. However, it is crucial for artists to critically engage with AI technology, ensuring that it remains a servant to human creativity rather than a replacement for it.

# CHAPTER 2: AI-GENERATED ART IN THE MUSIC INDUSTRY

In recent years, Artificial Intelligence (AI) has revolutionized various industries, and the music industry is no exception. AI has become a powerful tool that can blend creativity and technology, pushing the boundaries of what is possible in music composition. This subchapter explores the role of AI in music composition and its impact on the creative arts practitioners.

AI-generated art in the music industry has gained significant attention and appreciation. With the ability to analyze vast amounts of data and learn patterns, AI algorithms can compose original music, creating melodies, harmonies, and even lyrics. This technology allows creative arts practitioners to explore new horizons, experiment with different styles, and enhance their creativity. AI-generated music provides a fresh perspective, enabling musicians to explore uncharted territories and discover unique sounds.

Furthermore, AI can assist in the creative process by generating musical ideas and suggesting improvements to existing compositions. By analyzing a composer's previous works and understanding their style, AI algorithms can generate new musical ideas that align with the artist's preferences. This collaboration between human creativity and AI technology opens up new possibilities for musicians to explore and expand their artistic vision.

In addition to AI's role in music composition, its impact on photography and visual arts cannot be overlooked. AI algorithms can analyze images, identify patterns, and generate new visuals. From enhancing photographs to creating stunning visual effects, AI technology offers new tools for creative arts practitioners in the visual arts field. It allows photographers and visual artists to experiment with different styles, manipulate images, and create visually captivating artworks.

The integration of AI in the creative arts field brings both excitement and concerns. While AI provides new avenues for creativity, some argue that it may replace human artists. However, the true power lies in the collaboration between humans and AI. AI can assist artists, enhance their ideas, and provide new perspectives, but it cannot replace the human touch and emotions that are essential to art.

As creative arts practitioners, it is crucial to embrace the potential of AI in music composition and other art forms. By understanding the capabilities and limitations of AI technology, artists can leverage it as a tool to expand their creativity and explore new artistic territories. The collaboration between human creativity and AI technology holds great promise for the future of music composition and the wider creative arts industry.

In conclusion, AI's role in music composition is transforming the creative arts landscape. AI-generated art in the music industry opens up new possibilities and allows musicians to explore uncharted territories. Similarly, AI in photography and visual arts provides new tools for creative expression and experimentation. As creative arts practitioners, embracing the potential of AI can enhance our artistic vision and push the boundaries of what is possible in the world of art.

# AI-DRIVEN MUSIC PRODUCTION TECHNIQUES

In recent years, the integration of artificial intelligence (AI) in various industries has revolutionized the way we approach creativity and technology. The music industry is no exception. With the emergence of AI-driven music production techniques, creative arts practitioners are now exploring new realms of musical expression and pushing the boundaries of what is possible.

AI-generated art in the music industry has gained significant attention and has become a hot topic of discussion among musicians, producers, and enthusiasts. These AI-driven techniques enable artists to collaborate with intelligent algorithms that can compose melodies, harmonies, and even entire songs. By leveraging machine learning algorithms, AI can analyze vast amounts of music data, identifying patterns and structures that are not immediately apparent to humans. This allows for the creation of unique and innovative music compositions that would otherwise be difficult to conceive.

Additionally, AI in photography and visual arts has paved the way for the exploration of new creative possibilities. AI algorithms can analyze and understand visual data, allowing artists to generate stunning visual representations that were once only achievable through laborious manual processes. From generating intricate album covers to creating mesmerizing music videos, AI offers a wealth of opportunities for creative arts practitioners to enhance their visual storytelling and captivate audiences in new and exciting ways.

One of the most intriguing aspects of AI-driven music production techniques is the ability to blend human creativity with machine intelligence. While AI algorithms can generate musical ideas and even entire compositions, it is ultimately the role of the creative arts practitioner to curate, refine, and add their personal touch to the final product. This symbiotic relationship between human and machine opens up a whole new world of collaborative possibilities, enabling artists to explore uncharted territories and unlock their full creative potential.

However, as AI continues to advance in the music industry, questions surrounding originality and authenticity arise. Can AI-generated music be considered true art? Is it merely mimicking existing styles or creating something entirely new? These are important discussions that creative arts practitioners must engage in, as they navigate the ever-evolving landscape of AI-driven music production.

In conclusion, AI-driven music production techniques have paved the way for a new era of creativity and innovation in the music industry. From AI-generated compositions to visually stunning representations, artists can now explore uncharted territories and push the boundaries of their craft. However, it is crucial for creative arts practitioners to critically examine the role of AI in their work, ensuring that it enhances rather than diminishes their artistic vision. By embracing the possibilities offered by AI, creative arts practitioners can forge a new path that blends creativity and technology, elevating the art of music to new heights.

# AI-ENHANCED MUSIC PERFORMANCE AND INTERPRETATION

The integration of artificial intelligence (AI) into the creative arts industry has revolutionized the way we perceive and experience music. In this subchapter, we will delve into the world of AI-enhanced music performance and interpretation, exploring how this technology has shaped the landscape of the music industry. AI-generated art in the music industry has gained considerable traction in recent years. Through the use of sophisticated algorithms and machine learning techniques, AI systems can now compose original pieces of music that rival the work of human composers. These AI-generated compositions can be customized to fit various moods, genres, and even specific target audiences. The ability to produce music at such a scale has opened up new avenues for musicians, allowing them to explore uncharted territories and experiment with novel sounds and compositions.

Furthermore, AI has also proven instrumental in enhancing music interpretation. With the advancements in AI technology, musicians can now collaborate with intelligent systems that can analyze their performances in real-time and provide valuable feedback. This feedback can range from technical aspects, such as timing and intonation, to more nuanced elements, such as expression and interpretation.

By leveraging AI, musicians can refine their skills, push their boundaries, and gain new perspectives on their artistry.

The application of AI extends beyond music performance and interpretation and into the realms of photography and visual arts. Just as AI can generate music, it can also generate visual art, making it possible for AI systems to create stunning and captivating visuals.

Whether it is generating unique patterns, creating photo-realistic images, or even designing album covers, AI has become a valuable tool for photographers and visual artists to explore new horizons and push the boundaries of their craft.

However, it is important to note that while AI has undoubtedly brought about significant advancements in the creative arts industry, it should be viewed as a tool rather than a replacement for human creativity. AI systems are designed to augment and enhance the creative process, working in collaboration with human artists to produce extraordinary results. The fusion of human creativity and AI technology has the potential to unlock new levels of artistic expression and pave the way for groundbreaking innovations in the creative arts.

In conclusion, AI-enhanced music performance and interpretation have ushered in a new era for the creative arts industry. With the ability to generate music and provide real-time feedback, AI has revolutionized the way musicians approach their craft. Additionally, AI's impact extends beyond music and into photography and visual arts, enabling artists to create visually stunning works. By embracing AI as a tool, creative arts practitioners can tap into its immense potential to unlock new realms of artistic expression and push the boundaries of their creativity.

# Chapter 3: Exploring AI in Photography and Visual Arts
# The Intersection of AI and Photography

In recent years, the convergence of artificial intelligence (AI) and photography has brought about a revolutionary shift in the creative arts industry. This subchapter explores the profound impact of AI on photography and its wider implications for visual arts practitioners.

AI-generated art has already made significant inroads in the music industry, transforming the creative process and pushing the boundaries of what is possible. Similarly, AI in photography is revolutionizing the way we capture, manipulate, and appreciate visual imagery. Creative arts practitioners who embrace this technology can unlock new realms of artistic expression and expand their creative horizons. Artificial Intelligence in Music: Blending Creativity and Technology

Page 15

Artificial Intelligence in Music: Blending Creativity and Technology One of the most notable applications of AI in photography is the development of intelligent image recognition algorithms. These algorithms enable computers to analyze and understand the content of images, allowing for more accurate and efficient categorization, tagging, and searching of photographs. This breakthrough has revolutionized the way photographers organize and manage their vast collections of images, saving them time and effort in the process.

Moreover, AI has bestowed upon photographers the ability to enhance and manipulate images in ways that were previously unimaginable. By leveraging deep learning algorithms, photographers can now automatically enhance the quality of their photos, correct imperfections, and even add artistic filters with a single click. This not only streamlines the editing process but also allows for experimentation and the creation of unique visual styles.

AI-powered tools have also opened up new avenues for creative exploration in photography. Generative adversarial networks (GANs) are now capable of generating stunningly realistic images that blur the line between reality and fiction. Photographers can leverage these algorithms to create entirely new visual worlds, pushing the boundaries of their artistic vision.

While the integration of AI in photography offers immense creative potential, it also raises ethical and copyright concerns. As AI becomes more proficient at creating original works, questions arise regarding the ownership and authorship of AI-generated art. Furthermore, the potential for AI to manipulate and deceive through doctored or synthesized images is a pressing concern that must be addressed.

In conclusion, the intersection of AI and photography holds great promise for creative arts practitioners. By embracing AI-generated art in the music industry, photographers can tap into new realms of artistic expression. The integration of AI in photography allows for more efficient image management, streamlined editing processes, and the creation of previously unimaginable visual styles. However, it is crucial for practitioners to navigate the ethical implications and copyright concerns that arise with the use of AI in visual arts. As technology continues to evolve, creative arts practitioners must adapt and harness the power of AI to enhance their work while upholding ethical standards and protecting the integrity of their craft.

# AI-DRIVEN IMAGE ENHANCEMENT AND EDITING TOOLS

In recent years, the field of artificial intelligence (AI) has made significant advancements in various industries, including the creative arts. With the emergence of AI-driven image enhancement and editing tools, creative arts practitioners now have access to cutting-edge technologies that can revolutionize their work.

The music industry has always been at the forefront of innovation, constantly seeking new ways to captivate audiences and push artistic boundaries. AI-generated art is a prime example of this innovation. Using sophisticated algorithms, AI can analyze vast amounts of musical data to create unique compositions, melodies, and harmonies that were previously unimaginable.

These AI-generated compositions can serve as a source of inspiration for musicians, providing them with fresh ideas and new directions to explore in their creative process. Additionally, AI can assist in the production and mixing process by automatically enhancing audio quality, reducing noise, and balancing levels, ultimately leading to a more polished and professional sound.

Photography and visual arts are also witnessing the

transformative power of AI. AI- driven image enhancement tools allow photographers and visual artists to effortlessly improve the quality of their images.

These tools utilize machine learning algorithms to automatically enhance colors, adjust exposure, and sharpen details, resulting in stunning visuals. Furthermore, AI can be utilized in the editing process by automating time-consuming tasks such as background removal, object recognition, and even content generation. This not only saves artists valuable time but also provides them with the freedom to focus on the more creative aspects of their work.

However, like any technological advancement, AI-driven image enhancement and editing tools pose challenges and ethical considerations. These tools have the potential to devalue the human aspect of creativity and artistic expression. It is crucial for creative arts practitioners to strike a balance between utilizing AI as a tool and preserving their unique artistic vision and authenticity.

In conclusion, AI-driven image enhancement and editing tools have the potential to revolutionize the creative arts industry. Whether it be AI-generated music compositions or AI-assisted photography and visual arts, these tools offer innovative ways for creative arts practitioners to push the boundaries of their craft. It is essential for practitioners to embrace these advancements while also maintaining their individual artistic voices, ensuring that AI remains a powerful tool in their creative arsenal rather than overshadowing the human element of their work.

# AI FOR VISUAL ART GENERATION AND MANIPULATION

In recent years, artificial intelligence (AI) has revolutionized various industries, and the creative arts field is no exception. This subchapter delves into the fascinating world of AI for visual art generation and manipulation, exploring its applications in the music industry, photography, and visual arts.

The music industry has witnessed a significant transformation with the advent of AI- generated art. AI algorithms can now compose music, mimicking the styles of renowned artists or creating entirely new genres. These algorithms analyze vast amounts of musical data, identifying patterns and structures to generate original compositions. Creative arts practitioners can leverage this technology to explore new musical territories, pushing boundaries and expanding their artistic horizons.

Furthermore, AI has found its way into the realm of photography and visual arts. With AI-powered image recognition and analysis capabilities, artists can enhance their creative process and create visually striking pieces. AI algorithms can generate realistic images from scratch or manipulate existing ones to create unique visual experiences. This technology opens up a whole new realm of possibilities for creative arts practitioners, enabling them to experiment with different visual styles, explore surreal landscapes, or reimagine traditional art forms.

AI's ability to generate and manipulate visual art also brings forth ethical considerations and challenges. As creative arts practitioners, it is crucial to understand the balance between human creativity and AI assistance. While AI can provide new tools and inspiration, it should not replace the artist's personal touch and ingenuity. Artists must retain control over the artistic process and use AI as a tool to augment their creativity rather than overshadow it.

Moreover, the use of AI in the creative arts raises questions about originality and authenticity. As AI algorithms can analyze and mimic existing artistic styles, it becomes essential to consider the line between homage and plagiarism. Creative arts practitioners must navigate these ethical dilemmas, ensuring that their AI-generated art respects the work of others and maintains its unique value.

In conclusion, AI has become an exciting tool for visual art generation and manipulation in the creative arts field. Creative arts practitioners can leverage AI algorithms to explore new musical territories, experiment with visual styles, and push the boundaries of their artistic expression. However, it is crucial to strike a balance between human creativity and AI assistance, ensuring that the artist's personal touch and originality remain at the forefront. By embracing AI as a tool rather than a replacement, creative arts practitioners can harness its potential to create truly groundbreaking and innovative works of art.

# CHAPTER 4: BLENDING CREATIVITY AND TECHNOLOGY IN AI-GENERATED MUSIC

## The Creative Potential of AI-Generated Music

As creative arts practitioners, we constantly seek new avenues to push the boundaries of our craft. Artificial Intelligence (AI) has emerged as a powerful tool that not only enhances our artistic expressions but also introduces us to uncharted realms of creativity. In the music industry, AI-generated music has become a fascinating phenomenon, enabling us to explore unexplored sonic landscapes and challenge our traditional notions of composition and musicality.

AI-generated music is the result of algorithms and machine learning techniques that analyze vast amounts of musical data to generate compositions. This technology allows us to tap into an infinite pool of musical possibilities, transcending the limitations of our own human creativity. By leveraging AI in music production, we can expand our artistic horizons and create music that pushes the boundaries of traditional genres.

One of the most exciting aspects of AI-generated music is its ability to capture and mimic the stylistic nuances of different artists and genres. For example, AI algorithms can analyze the works of Mozart or Bach and generate new compositions that encapsulate their distinct musical styles. This opens up a world of possibilities for artists to collaborate with legendary musicians of the past or to create entirely new genres by blending different styles.

Moreover, AI-generated music can serve as a source of inspiration for creative arts practitioners working in other mediums, such as photography and visual arts. Just as AI has transformed the music industry, it is also revolutionizing the way we approach visual aesthetics. AI algorithms can analyze visual data and generate images that mimic the styles of renowned artists or create entirely new visual compositions. This cross- pollination of AI-generated art in the music industry, photography, and visual arts can lead to exciting collaborations and new artistic expressions that were previously unimaginable.

However, it is important to remember that AI-generated music is not a replacement for human creativity but rather a tool to enhance it. As creative arts practitioners, we bring our unique sensibilities, emotions, and experiences to the artistic process. AI-generated music can assist us in exploring new creative territories, but it is our own interpretation and human touch that give it life and meaning.

In conclusion, the creative potential of AI-generated music is immense. It offers us a gateway to unexplored sonic landscapes, the ability to collaborate with legendary musicians of the past, and inspiration for cross-disciplinary artistic expressions. As creative arts practitioners, embracing AI in our artistic journey can lead to groundbreaking innovations and redefine the boundaries of our craft. Let us harness the power of AI to blend creativity and technology, creating a new era of artistic possibilities.

# COLLABORATIONS BETWEEN AI AND HUMAN MUSICIANS

In recent years, the field of artificial intelligence (AI) has made significant advancements in various industries, including the creative arts. This subchapter explores the exciting collaborations between AI and human musicians, showcasing how the blending of creativity and technology is reshaping the music industry.

AI-generated art in the music industry has emerged as a powerful tool for musicians, composers, and producers. AI algorithms can analyze vast amounts of musical data, enabling them to generate new compositions, improvisations, and even harmonies that are indistinguishable from those created by human musicians. This technology has opened up a world of possibilities for musicians, allowing them to explore new musical landscapes and push the boundaries of traditional composition.

Moreover, AI has the ability to analyze and learn from existing musical works, allowing it to compose music in various genres and styles. Collaborating with AI can provide human musicians with fresh perspectives, inspiring them to experiment with new and unconventional musical elements that they may not have considered before. This fusion of AI and human creativity can result in truly unique and groundbreaking compositions.

Beyond music, AI has also found its place in the visual arts, including photography and visual arts. AI algorithms can analyze vast databases of images, enabling them to generate stunning visual compositions, mimic artistic styles, and even create entirely new visual concepts. Many photographers and visual artists have embraced AI technology as a means of enhancing their creative process, enabling them to explore new aesthetics and experiment with different visual techniques.

The collaborations between AI and human musicians present both exciting opportunities and challenges. On the one hand, AI can provide invaluable assistance to creative arts practitioners, offering them new tools and sources of inspiration. On the other hand, concerns about AI replacing human creativity persist. However, it is essential to view AI as a complement to human creativity rather than a replacement. AI can enhance and amplify human artistic expression, but it cannot replicate the deeply emotional and subjective aspects of human creativity.

In conclusion, collaborations between AI and human musicians are revolutionizing the music industry and creative arts as a whole. The integration of AI-generated art in the music industry and the use of AI in photography and visual arts have opened up new possibilities for creative exploration. By embracing AI as a partner, creative arts practitioners can push the boundaries of their own creativity, creating art that combines the best of human and machine ingenuity.

# ETHICAL AND LEGAL CONSIDERATIONS IN AI-GENERATED MUSIC

As artificial intelligence (AI) continues to revolutionize various creative industries, including music, it becomes crucial for creative arts practitioners to understand and address the ethical and legal considerations surrounding AI-generated music. In this subchapter, we delve into the implications and challenges associated with AI-generated music, specifically targeting the audience of creative arts practitioners, with a focus on AI-generated art in the music industry, AI in photography, and visual arts.

One of the primary ethical concerns surrounding AI-generated music revolves around the issue of authorship and ownership. With AI algorithms capable of composing intricate music pieces, questions arise as to who should be credited as the creator of the music. Should it be the AI algorithms, the developers, or the artist who curates and refines the generated compositions? Addressing this issue requires a thoughtful examination of intellectual property rights, copyright laws, and a reevaluation of conventional notions of creativity and originality.

Another ethical consideration is the potential impact on human musicians and composers. As AI-generated music becomes more sophisticated and accessible, there is a concern that it may devalue the work of human musicians and replace their roles in the industry. Striking a balance between AI-generated music and human creativity is crucial to ensure the preservation of artistic integrity and diversity in the music landscape.

Furthermore, there are legal considerations related to the use of AI-generated music in commercial and public domains. Licensing and royalty distribution become complex when AI-generated compositions are involved. Determining the fair compensation for AI-generated music and the rights of human musicians working alongside AI systems requires clear legal frameworks that are yet to be fully developed.

In addition to ethical and legal considerations, the subchapter also explores the potential applications of AI in photography and visual arts. AI algorithms are already capable of creating stunning visual artworks and enhancing photographers' creative process.

However, this raises questions about the authenticity and integrity of the art form. How does AI-generated art challenge traditional artistic practices and aesthetics? What are the implications for the role of photographers and visual artists in this evolving landscape?

In conclusion, as AI-generated music, photography, and visual arts continue to shape the creative industry, it is essential for creative arts practitioners to navigate the ethical and legal considerations associated with this emerging technology. Balancing the benefits of AI with the preservation of human creativity and addressing issues of authorship, ownership, and fair compensation are critical to ensure a sustainable and inclusive future for AI in the creative arts.

# CHAPTER 5: CHALLENGES AND OPPORTUNITIES IN AI- DRIVEN ART

## Overcoming Bias and Limitations in AI-Generated Art

In recent years, the integration of artificial intelligence (AI) in various creative fields, including music, photography, and visual arts, has sparked a wave of excitement and innovation. AI-generated art has the potential to push boundaries, challenge conventional thinking, and inspire new forms of creativity. However, like any emerging technology, AI has its limitations and biases that must be addressed in order to fully realize its potential.

One of the primary challenges in AI-generated art is overcoming bias. AI algorithms are trained using vast amounts of data, which can inadvertently encode biases present in the training dataset. This can result in AI-generated art that perpetuates stereotypes, discriminates against certain groups, or lacks diversity. It is essential for creative arts practitioners to be aware of these biases and actively work towards mitigating them.

To overcome bias in AI-generated art, it is crucial to diversify the training data. By including a wide range of voices, perspectives, and cultural backgrounds, we can ensure that the AI algorithms are exposed to a more comprehensive and inclusive dataset. Additionally, incorporating human oversight and intervention in the creative process can help identify and correct any biased outputs generated by the AI.

Furthermore, limitations in AI-generated art should also be acknowledged and addressed. While AI algorithms have shown remarkable advancements in generating music, photography, and visual art, they still struggle with certain aspects of creativity. AI may excel in replicating existing styles or patterns, but it often struggles to generate truly original and groundbreaking art. Creative arts practitioners should view AI as a tool to enhance their own creativity rather than a replacement for their artistic skills.

In the music industry, AI-generated art can be utilized to automate certain repetitive tasks, such as composing background melodies or generating chord progressions. However, it is important to remember that the emotional depth and authenticity of music come from human experiences and expressions. AI can augment and inspire, but it cannot fully replace the human touch.

Similarly, in photography and visual arts, AI can assist in tasks like image enhancement, style transfer, or even generating new visual compositions. However, the artistic vision and intent behind a photograph or artwork are deeply rooted in human perception and interpretation. AI can provide new tools and techniques, but the final artistic decisions should always be made by the creative arts practitioners themselves.

In conclusion, AI-generated art has immense potential in the creative arts industry, but it comes with its own set of limitations and biases. By actively working to overcome bias, diversifying training data, and acknowledging the limitations of AI, creative arts practitioners can harness the power of AI to enhance their creativity and push the boundaries of artistic expression. AI should be viewed as a powerful tool to amplify human creativity rather than a replacement for it.

# EXPLORING NEW AVENUES FOR CREATIVITY THROUGH AI

In recent years, the rapid advancements in artificial intelligence (AI) have not only transformed various industries but have also made a significant impact on the creative arts. From AI-generated art in the music industry to AI in photography and visual arts, the integration of technology and creativity has opened up new avenues for artistic expression and innovation.

One of the most fascinating developments in the music industry is the emergence of AI- generated music. With AI algorithms trained on vast datasets of existing music, machines are now capable of composing original pieces that rival the creativity of human artists. This revolutionary technology has not only challenged traditional notions of authorship and creativity but has also expanded the possibilities of musical composition. AI-generated music can inspire musicians, provide them with new ideas, and even collaborate with them in real-time, pushing the boundaries of what is musically possible.

Similarly, AI has made significant strides in photography and visual arts. With the help of machine learning algorithms, AI can now analyze and understand visual content, allowing it to generate highly realistic and aesthetically pleasing images. This technology has proven to be particularly useful in tasks such as image restoration, style transfer, and even the creation of entirely new artworks. AI tools can assist photographers and visual artists by automating time-consuming tasks, enhancing image quality, and providing them with fresh perspectives and artistic inspiration.

While some may argue that AI-generated art lacks the emotional depth and human touch of traditional artistic creations, it is crucial to recognize that AI is not here to replace human creativity but to augment it. By enabling artists to explore new possibilities and experiment with unconventional techniques, AI serves as a powerful tool in the hands of creative arts practitioners.

However, it is important to approach AI in the creative arts with a sense of responsibility and ethics. As technology continues to advance, it is essential to ensure that AI- generated art respects copyright laws, promotes diversity, and does not perpetuate harmful biases. Striking a balance between human intuition and machine intelligence is the key to harnessing the true potential of AI in the creative arts.

In conclusion, the integration of AI in the creative arts, specifically in the music industry and photography/visual arts, has opened up exciting new avenues for innovation and artistic expression. AI-generated music and visuals can inspire and collaborate with artists, pushing the boundaries of what is creatively possible. However, it is crucial to approach AI in the creative arts responsibly, ensuring ethical practices and maintaining the unique human touch that defines the creative process. By embracing AI as a tool and exploring its potential, creative arts practitioners can unlock new realms of creativity and reshape the future of their respective industries.

# FUTURE POSSIBILITIES AND TRENDS IN AI-DRIVEN ART

Artificial Intelligence (AI) has revolutionized various industries, and the creative arts field is no exception. As technology continues to advance, AI-driven art is becoming increasingly prevalent, offering new possibilities and trends for creative arts practitioners. This subchapter explores the future of AI-generated art in the music industry, as well as its implications for photography and visual arts.

AI-generated art in the music industry is rapidly evolving, offering exciting opportunities for musicians, producers, and composers. One of the most significant advancements is the ability of AI systems to compose original music. Through machine learning algorithms, AI can analyze vast amounts of musical data, identify patterns, and generate new compositions based on these insights. This technology enables artists to explore new genres, experiment with unconventional song structures, and push the boundaries of creativity. Furthermore, AI can assist in the production process by automatically generating harmonies, melodies, and even lyrics, providing artists with a wealth of inspiration and accelerating the creative workflow.

In photography and visual arts, AI has also made remarkable strides. AI-powered algorithms can now analyze and generate realistic images, mimicking the style of famous artists or creating entirely new ones. Artists can use AI as a tool to enhance their creative process, generating ideas or even collaborating with AI systems to co- create unique pieces. Additionally, AI can automate repetitive tasks, such as image editing or retouching, allowing artists to focus more on conceptualization and experimentation. This fusion of AI and visual arts opens up a world of possibilities, enabling artists to explore new aesthetic realms and challenge traditional artistic boundaries.

Looking ahead, the future of AI-driven art holds even greater potential. As technology continues to advance, AI systems will become more sophisticated, capable of understanding and replicating human emotions, preferences, and intentions. This opens up possibilities for creating personalized and interactive art experiences, where AI systems can generate art that resonates with individuals on a deeply emotional level. Imagine attending a concert where an AI system dynamically adjusts the music based on the audience's mood or interacting with a virtual art installation that responds to your emotions in real-time. The integration of AI into the creative arts field has the potential to create immersive and transformative experiences for both artists and audiences alike.

In conclusion, AI-driven art is revolutionizing the creative arts industry, offering new possibilities and trends for creative arts practitioners. From AI-generated music to AI- assisted photography and visual arts, the fusion of AI and creativity is pushing the boundaries of artistic expression. As technology continues to advance, the future of AI- driven art holds even greater potential for creating personalized and interactive art experiences that resonate deeply with individuals. Embracing AI as a tool in the creative process can unlock new realms of creativity and push the boundaries of what is possible in the world of art.

In our discussions, we have uncovered several key insights:

1. AI is a powerful tool for augmenting human creativity rather than replacing it. The symbiotic relationship between AI and human artists is the key to unlocking new artistic possibilities.

2. Ethical considerations surrounding AI-generated art are crucial. As AI becomes more prevalent in the creative process, we must carefully navigate issues such as copyright, ownership, and the role of human artists in the creative equation.

3. Collaboration between AI and human artists can result in groundbreaking and innovative creations. By embracing AI, creative practitioners can explore uncharted territories and challenge traditional artistic conventions.

4. AI can help democratize the creative arts by providing accessible tools and platforms for aspiring artists. This inclusivity allows for a broader range of voices and perspectives in the art world.

In conclusion, our exploration of AI-generated art in the music industry, as well as AI in photography and visual arts, has revealed a multitude of exciting possibilities. The integration of AI into the creative process offers new avenues for artistic expression and challenges traditional norms. As creative arts practitioners, embracing AI can enhance our creativity, expand our horizons, and empower us to shape the future of the arts.

# THE FUTURE OF AI IN THE CREATIVE ARTS

As technology continues to advance at an unprecedented rate, the creative arts industry finds itself at the forefront of embracing Artificial Intelligence (AI) in various forms. From AI-generated art in the music industry to AI in photography and visual arts, the possibilities seem endless.

In the music industry, AI has already begun to revolutionize the way music is composed, produced, and consumed. With the help of sophisticated algorithms and machine learning techniques, AI can generate music that rivals the creativity and emotional depth of human composers. AI systems can analyze vast amounts of musical data, identify patterns, and generate original compositions that are both technically impressive and aesthetically pleasing.

Imagine a future where AI can compose music tailored to individual preferences, taking into account personal tastes, moods, and even physiological responses. AI-generated music could create a deeply immersive and personalized experience for listeners, enhancing emotional connections and pushing the boundaries of creativity.
But would a consumer of art be satisfied with their own creation? Consumers of music and art bond with creators, finding specific individuals captivating and seductive. When a client commissions an artwork, they buy a part of the creator. They

bond with the maker.

AI would need to create itself into a marketable and lovable character in the way that Disney has bonded with children. Starting a fan base with children is something that AI could do easily through cartoons and tunes and is already doing.

The AI branded construct (we must distinguish between the broad term and the creative entity that AI has enabled) now becomes a new organic concept. This is not new phenomenon. Nike and Disney might be considered forerunners. Brands are more similar to the concept of a character styled AI than we might think.

This ties in with the idea that the work of Banksy or Salvador Dali which, no matter what it is, will sell at the highest of current art prices, because of the name, the brand, and of course, the investment possibilities.

Could AI art ever be an investment? Not unless it were to brand itself accordingly and in a creative way and this we know is down to humans.


©2024 Sarnia de la Mare/Tale Teller Club

www.taletellerclub.com

Sarnia de la Maré FRSA is a composer, author and artist with the Tale Teller Club

# ABOUT THE AUTHOR

**Sarnia De La Mare**

Sarnia de la Mare FRSA is an author, composer, and artist with the Tale Teller Club Academy of Arts and a member of the Tale Teller Club Band and orchestra.

Primarily writing science fiction novels,  The Book of Immersion Series and others.

Sarnia is also a keen explorer of AI and what it means in an egalitarian world. This book is part of a series called The Humanitarian AI.

www.ingramcontent.com/pod-product-compliance
Lightning Source LLC
Chambersburg PA
CBHW070226260726
48658CB00006BA/2186